Walking Out of Brokenness into Wholeness

Shelia M. Walker

ENTEGRITY
CHOICE PUBLISHING

Entegrity Choice Publishing
PO Box 453
Powder Springs, GA 30127
info@entegritypublishing.com
www.entegritypublishing.com
770.727.6517

Printed in the United States of America

Library of Congress Cataloging-in-Publication Data
ISBN 979-8-9850792-0-3
Library of Congress Control Number: 2021920618

Contents

Acknowledgements

Above all, I thank God for being my greatest love. He gave me the strength to complete this endeavor.

I cannot express my appreciation for the unconditional support of my committed and loving husband, Lee Walker, Sr.

I am grateful for my insightful friends, relatives, and others who have tirelessly supported me, both personally and professionally.

Introduction

A dear friend and sister came by my house one evening and brought me a gift for my birthday. We laughed and talked for a while, and then the conversation changed. She asked me, "Shelia, why are you waiting so long to write that book that God told you to write a long time ago?" I got quiet because my husband had asked me that same question the night before. This was no coincidence; this was confirmation. I thought nothing of it, until the realization kicked in that I knew it was time for me to stop ignoring what God had told me to do years ago. I simply needed to surrender to the plans that were designed for me by God to do His will. It was time to move forward. How can I be so selfish to not share my life story to help others?

Now that I am on this journey, I believe that it is my mission and purpose to share with the world that we will face many obstacles in our lives, but we can overcome them. Our past does not define us. People are going to talk no matter what, whether it's good or bad. It took me a while to love those who have hated me without reason; I could never understand why. It is not always easy when your faith is under fire. I refuse to gravitate to self-pity and shame, but into a motivator of myself, loving who had finally accepted ME.

I will never hide the talents that the Lord has given me. No longer will insecurity rule my life. If it makes some feel uncomfortable for me to talk about the many blessings that God has given me, do me a favor and have a cup of coffee on me. Remember this: whatever you are lacking in your life, God will provide, even when others feel you are unworthy of HIS blessings.

No one said you must have a PhD to live a good life, but having an education provides the power and ability to succeed and achieve your life goals. I earned my GED, graduated from Mississippi College with a bachelor's degree in Sociology and a minor in Psychology, and am graduating from Jackson State University with a master's degree in Clinical Mental Health. Praise God! I am on the right path that will push me forward to my destiny!

Growing up, my childhood was dark, limited, and unsure. Without the stability of a two-parent home, my early years of life were not protected from those I thought were supposed to love and guide me into womanhood with the knowledge of the dos and don'ts of being a woman. Hopefully, after reading this book, you will know that you can overcome hurt, rejection, lies, and not feeling loved.

1

Stepping Out of Brokenness into Wholeness

There is an answer, and his name is JESUS. Getting to know Him has kept me from losing my mind and committing suicide. I became a mother at fifteen. This was mainly because I was never taught about sex. I had always listened to a neighborhood friend who was older and never meant me any good, and of course I was too blind to see that. I tried to fit in anywhere I could find love and acceptance. I became pregnant a second time, blending into what I saw in my family and women in the neighborhood who became pregnant just to collect checks and live off the system. I'm not saying that was the case for everyone; some of the women did work and strive to better their lives.

What I am saying is, how can a child see her mother with different male companions in the house without thinking this was a normal way of life? I grew up seeing this. I was told on many occasions that I was going to be just like my mother: an apartment full of kids from different fathers. Let me tell you, I started off just like that. I felt as though I was heading in the same direction as my mother. I tried to go to school but could not because my mother was receiving government assistance for her children, and there were many bills that had to be paid. In addition to receiving a welfare check and food stamps, my mother had to pay for her medicine. If there was no money left for her to get her medicine, my uncle Otha would pay for her medicine. My home life was a disaster. Now that I have lived through that period in my life, I have come to realize that my mother did what she could with what she had. I recall a time when things at home had gotten so bad that my sister began shoplifting and doing whatever she could to survive. She stole clothes so she could have something to wear to school. My sister was arrested on many occasions for shoplifting and other things that teenagers get into trouble for. Once, without my sister's permission, I wore some of her clothes to school because I had nothing to wear. When I came home from school, my sister jumped on me for wearing her clothes. She failed to realize that all I wanted to do was to look decent and not have my classmates laughing at me. My shoes were also extremely worn-out. After that incident, I vowed never to go to school again. I felt so rejected and most of all unloved. I did not go to school for a while, but later realized that you cannot stay in your own mess and wallow in it, so I decided to change.

I have always had a fighting spirit because I was determined to make it somehow without following in my mother's footsteps. I left home at the age of 17 with a limited education and no job skills. Many of the people my sister had gone to school with were into prostitution. I knew that lifestyle would not be a way out for me. Stuck in what seemed like a world of despair after I left home, my mother suffered a mental breakdown and had to go to the hospital. I went to live with my aunt Mary. I will always be grateful to her for taking me in.

Aunt Mary taught me things that I should have been taught at home, but never was. I had an "a-ha" moment one day when it dawned on me: "How can my mother teach and train me when it was never taught to her?" This moment of realization caused me to adjust my attitude and outlook. This is when the sun began to shine through my darkness.

As early as age 10 (4th grade), I spent my summers with Aunt Mary. She allowed me to be myself and she provided for me as if I was her child. She took me to church every Sunday. When I would go to Vacation Bible School, she would say, "You learn everything you can and hold onto what has been taught, because you never know when and where you will have to pray." She told me to always keep JESUS in my heart no matter how dark life seemed. "Remember, Jesus is the light."

When I was with Aunt Mary, we would talk and laugh for hours. She would do just about anything to get me to smile and laugh. She said I had the funniest laugh she had ever heard. At the time, I did not know that God placed me in her home so that she could introduce me to a Savior who loves me unconditionally. I also learned that my sins could be forgiven. I must admit, Aunt Mary did all that she could to keep and raise me.

Aunt Mary told me when I felt weary to read Psalms 23 and meditate on the Word of God. I wished that my summers would last forever with her; I hated for them to end. I did not want to return to the chaos at home. The time I spent with Aunt Mary seemed to give me what I needed to face the challenges that were before me.

I found out later in life that you must get to know God for yourself. Although I had four other brothers and two sisters, each of them decided they would leave home at eighteen and make a better life for themselves, and they did. I was left to take care of myself, my mother, and two brothers, who later had to be taken care of by another aunt. I was furious when my older siblings left home. I thought it was selfish that they left me and my younger brothers at home with my mother because of her mental state. I asked my oldest sister if I could come and live with her, and she said no. My sister told me she was getting married and needed to start her own life and that she did not have time to raise me or anyone else. I cried as my heart felt as if it was broken into a million pieces. She showed no remorse and did not care.

I kept trying to come to terms with her decision. From my viewpoint, I could not understand how she could be so cold, knowing the condition that we were left in. I felt lost and abandoned, and the rejection that I felt as a child seemed to be coming back. I guess my sister was trying to tell me, "Each person for themselves, so figure life out for yourself."

I was looking for a savior in my older sisters and brothers, but to this day my sister is still that selfish person who only thinks about herself. Never once did she offer any money to help us out; however, she did call when she needed to borrow money for rent or to make a car payment.

I asked my sister, "How is it that you were not willing to give to your own flesh and blood in their time of need?" Those needs were not only financial, but love, patience, and understanding. I reminded her of how she abandoned me and my other siblings with no regrets. She responded, "It was not my job to raise you all when you had a mother to do it." When she needed help, I had no reservations about helping her. I wanted her to realize that she was selfish. She was so selfish that she did not attend her own mother's funeral. Her excuse was, "I am not coming back to Mississippi." She said that the reason she did not want to come back was that someone stole money from her when she visited. She felt that I should be the one responsible for paying it back since I was the executor over my mother's affairs. My response to her was, "I am not paying money back that I did not take." I firmly believe that we reap what we have sown. This thought came to mind, "How many times have God's children stolen from HIM?"

Nevertheless, my sister has been known to use drugs, which may have altered her thinking. She had no proof that anyone took her money. This excuse should not have caused her to miss her mother's funeral and not be there to support the family during our time of grief. My sister and I are like strangers, although we share the same mother and father. We share no commonalities, except through birth. I have tried many times to reach out to her, but get no response. Regardless, whether she ever accepts me or not, there will always be love for her in my heart. It hurts that she never got the opportunity to know her youngest sister. I will continue to pray that she has a change of heart and will eventually get to know her family.

2

The Accused

I have never been to prison physically, but I have mentally. No one will ever understand the stress that I endured when my older sisters and brothers left home. My body was going through a tremendous amount of stress and fatigue, so much so that I began to lose my hair. I had to be put on medication to control my crying spells. Life did not seem livable. Satan wanted my life, and I almost gave up and turned away from my love for the Lord. Trust me, your mind is a battleground for Satan to play on. Doubting God was a no-no for me. Although the devil has tried and is still trying, my faith kept me from having a mental breakdown. There were so many issues in my life, the fleshly part of me felt as if I wanted to give up and turn back to the world.

As long as I was serving Satan and not God the issues were there, but never presented themselves. I was not praying and did not care because in my foolish thinking, I thought I could fix my own problems. Let me tell you, I was wrong and I knew it, but I was not ready to commit my life to Christ. I had some knowledge of

God because my aunt had shared Christ with me and that was it. Learning about God is like being a newborn baby who starts out by drinking milk, then slowly graduates to eating food.

This is what made me change my life. I was assaulted by a friend that I considered to be a brother. He choked me and left me for dead. I never told anyone because I was ashamed and believed it was my fault. I held that traumatic experience in for many years. I came to realize that I did not want to die like that, without being saved. Sometimes, it takes drastic things to happen to change our life. I thank God I did not die in my sins, and He gave me another chance to turn my life around. After that experience, I accepted Christ; I thought it was going to be a cakewalk, but I was wrong about that too. It looked like troubles were coming from every direction, starting with losing my job. My children started acting up one by one. When one child got straightened out, then the other siblings would follow suit. When I thought things could not get any worse, I suffered the loss of my mother, a brother, and a sister. On top of all of that, I was summoned to court based on false accusations alleged by members of my own family.

On the day of court, I walked boldly into the courtroom with a smile on my face and asked the judge, "What am I being accused of?" The judge answered, "You are being accused of conspiracy to commit peace, moving the family's church memberships, dividing up the family, and not attending family gatherings. How do you plea?" My response was, "Not guilty."

He asked again, "What is your plea?" I responded, "Not guilty" While being respectful and with confidence in my voice, I asked, "What is it about 'not guilty' that you do not understand and why do you feel the need to repeat the question?" The judge answered, "I wanted to make sure you heard me." I told him I heard him the first time. He sternly stated, "Young lady, do you know that I will hold you in contempt of court?" I told him to go ahead. I will not be alone.

My display of self-confidence was present because I had God as my attorney, and my accusers had Satan as their attorney. I must admit, I was a bit annoyed by my accusers thinking the judge was on their side and I was going to be convicted. In my mind, I had my hands held high praising my Heavenly Father. I had faith and confidence that there was no way I could be found guilty of such absurd and false accusations by my own family.

My accusers eagerly awaited the answer from the judge. They felt they had me right where they wanted me. I stood with a smile on my face when the judge announced that I was innocent of all their accusations. You see, I was not worried about what man could do to me. One thing I know for sure is that you can kill my body, but not my soul. God is always on time, and He delivered me out of the hands of my enemies. The lesson here is to never accuse anyone of anything unless you have proof. Being falsely accused can lead you to being laughed at in your face. Satan, you have been defeated!

My accusers were unable to understand my radiance. They only saw the darkness that Satan allowed them to see. It is sad because this is what they wanted to see. God allows my cheerful and optimistic nature to shine because I am a servant of God. God's assurance to me is written in Matthew 5:11: "Blessed are you when others revile you, and persecute you, and utter all kinds of evil against you, for my name's sake." Thank God for allowing me to overcome and rise above the negativity.

3

Who's Fooling Who?

How is it that you are expected to give love and respect when it is not given to you? It's as if it is owed to them and it is, but on the other hand, you are not worth what is required of them to give, which is the same thing that they want from you. Some people try hard to hide their undercover falseness and lying lips, pretending that their love for you is real when all you see from a spiritual standpoint is deception. I blame myself for giving my heart to those who continued to break it, but not anymore. I realize that my heart was broken, so I made a conscious decision to stop giving my heart to those who enjoyed getting the pleasure of doing so, and now I have a clear understanding of why my heart never healed. Simply, my heart never healed because I wanted the people who were continuously hurting me in my life when God had separated me from them. At the time, I just did not understand. Hatred and bitterness exist, but the most dangerous one of all is generational curses of unforgiveness.

For many years, I overlooked the truth of how things

can change if some have not accepted Jesus Christ. The scales are off now, and my vision is clear. I have come to terms with myself. I cannot force anyone to love, accept, and respect me, whether its friends or family. Through these difficult and trying experiences, the lessons were for me to change, not for me to try to change someone else.

True love does not come from man; it comes from the Lord. My focus is to not allow those to infiltrate back in my life, knowing their focus is to continue to hurt me. Their goal is to make only themselves feel good. Instead of coming to me saying, "I am sorry," they said, "If I have offended you." They used the word "if" because what they were really saying was, they doubt they did anything to hurt me.

You should never allow someone else's bitterness to weigh on you. God will keep you in spite of attacks from others. Be careful about crushing someone's spirit because you can leave them spiritually damaged. When you do this, you bring damnation upon yourself. No longer do I cry for those who do not accept me. It has been a pleasure walking away from people that I allowed to attach themselves to me because of my insecurities.

For years, I was like a little girl who was crying inside and never healed. What I was overlooking is that I had attached myself to those I felt would validate me. Often times God showed me warning signs, but I ignored them and did the opposite. Thank you, Lord, for chastising me with your love and revealing those who are wolves in sheep clothing. I will no longer go down the road that almost led me to death. It is all right to separate yourself from toxic people who cause you pain, even if it is your family.

True change comes from within, and you need God's help to achieve this change. God's love is real. God is not the author of confusion, but of peace. Protect your peace and look out for people if you know their only purpose is to cause division. I was fooled for a long time. Take it from me: stop looking at their face because that face is familiar and you can be easily misled; instead, look at their character and behavior.

One must learn to make wise decisions for who should be a part of their life. Surround yourself with people who can deposit good things into your life, not drain you spiritually and emotionally. Stay away from joy SNATCHERS! Through it all, my Father stayed close to me; HE is the only one that can heal a broken heart.

"O taste and see that the Lord is good: blessed is the man that trust in him." Psalms 34:8

Like many of you, I had put my trust in the wrong hands. I used to ask God, "Why me?" On the other hand, "Why not me?" God used me for others to see him at work in me, so that others could believe and be saved. Sometimes, you have to be taken out of your comfort zone and put in an uncomfortable place to realize that you have been comfortable too long. God will test our resolve at times. He will place us in a position and we will have to decide if we will trust Him or give up. God said He will never leave us or forsake us. He did not say that he would keep us from storms, but that HE will be with us while we are going through the storms of life. Remember, rainbows come at the end of a storm and there is light at the end of every tunnel.

4

When God Is Pushing You into Your Destiny

There were many scriptures that Jesus used when He was accused of not being the Savior. Today, Satan still plants seeds of doubt in our lives about who we are. Some people have displayed a negative attitude towards me because I am in God's favor. In my weakness, I rejected God's favor to please man. It was more important for me at that time to go along, because I did not feel that I deserved God's love. I ran away from my Father's blessings.

I was in this dark place for years. God's word will draw you close to Him or drive you away from Him. I was already living in my own personal hell, thinking to myself, "Are you a soldier for the Lord or a coward?" Examining and thinking about all that He had done for me and my family, I made the decision that I am going to be a soldier. I had to come out of self-pity. In order for me to come out, I learned how to pray and ask God, "If it be your will, let it be done. Most of all, Lord, order my footsteps so when I fall, you and you alone will give me the strength to stand and put my faith in drive and go forward for the plans you have designed for me, and I shall be obedient and praise Your Holy name.

God knew that I had some work to do, and He let me know that He does not need my "stop and go" faith. The Lord let me see that I would only draw close to him when my cup was empty and need filling again. I was running to the Lord only when I needed to get a cup of faith "to go." As my relationship with Jesus Christ began to grow through the Word of God, I learned that He is the living water and that I would never be thirsty if I surrendered to His will.

When I truly surrendered my life to Him, I no longer had "stop and go" faith. God's well never runs dry, and His word is always with me. There were times when people would say to me, "I wish I had what you have" with a devilish look on their face and praying idolatrous prayers unto the Lord, like, "Lord bless me with what she has." You must stop praying for what God has blessed someone else with and start praying that God renews your mind and soul to be changed from an idol worshiper to being a true worshiper of Christ. It is all right to be happy for others, celebrate with them and rejoice, but we must recognize that all good and perfect gifts come from the Lord and not man.

Now that I am on this journey, it is my mission and purpose to share with the world that God is with you when you face obstacles in your life. It is not always easy when your faith is tested and it seems as if no one understands you. It is not that they should understand; it is understanding who Christ has called you to be. Whatever you are lacking in your life God will provide, especially when others feel you are unworthy of His blessings.

One Sunday at church - yes, I said church - a member approached me and asked about the car that I had gotten for my 40th birthday. She asked several people that day what type of education I had to allow me to drive a new car - especially that type of car. For some reason, she believed that I was not supposed to be driving that kind of car. What she failed to realize is that others saw her jealousy. I looked at her and laughed, because I knew this was an attempt by the devil to make me feel unworthy.

Whether you eat with the prince or the potter, you are still who God says you are. Stop chasing other people's dreams and figure out what God is saying to you about your life. I thank God for those special people in my life, and no matter what time of day or night that I may need them, they are there for me.

5

In-law Conflict

I met my husband almost 40 years ago at a friend's house; the friend was his cousin. We began dating and later married. I am grateful to God for sending me a man who accepted my two children. We had three more children and became a blended family. Please do not think that it did not come without a price. I had family members who told my children that my husband is not their father and they do not have to obey him. Those negative family members placed a strain on my husband's relationship with my two older children, and they carried their resentment into adulthood. They looked at their siblings as my husband's kids. They took bad family advice and made all kinds of accusations against him.

It is a funny thing now that I look back and see the work of Satan. It started with me in my mother's womb being born prematurely. My father's family never acknowledged me as his child. When my troubles began, I realized that Satan's mission is to steal, kill, and destroy. Trust me when I say Satan wanted to kill me because he knows the life God has planned for me.

Some of you may want to know how my husband and I dealt with all the turmoil that was going on. Now let me tell you how we dealt with family. We continued to pray, and God gave us strength to fight and call the enemy out and serve him notice that we were not going to be defeated. At that time, we were being attacked on all sides; both our families and the children were acting out and being rebellious. There were times when we wanted to throw in the towel. I asked my husband, "Baby, why are we hated so much?"

Things had gotten so bad with our children that they started calling our pastor to talk to him about us. I recall a church member approaching me and asking questions - as if she were the police and I was the suspect being interrogated - on church grounds. One of the things she asked me was what were we doing to make our children want to leave home. I respectfully pointed out to her, "When our children came to you, you should have told them what the Bible says about being obedient to parents." I went on to tell her how she provided them with the idea that it was okay for them to leave home and enjoy their lives.

We told our children that they were going to church and that they would work in the church. You would think an elderly Christian woman sitting on the Mother's Board would advise your children to do the right things in life and obey their parents. However, this woman lacked wisdom. That is why it is so important to

look at who your role models are. One could get hood-
winked by thinking he or she is a person filled with
wisdom and knowledge, but their hearts are far from it.
When my children received what I knew was bad advice
I told them, "Do not leave home thinking that you are
grown, staying out late and partying, and come home
when you get ready, because that is not acceptable at
this house."

It is disturbing to witness an aged person being bitter and messy. It is important for mothers-in-law on
both sides not to get involved with parents raising their
children when their values and morals are different
from yours. Of course, that is what happens when you
are on two different pages of life on how to parent and
properly raise children.

My children talked with their grandparents, thinking
the standards and expectations from their parents were
going to change. Our parenting decisions for our children did not change. Today, I am a grandparent myself
and God knows I love my grandchildren, but my sons
and daughters' children know they cannot come to me
or my husband and talk about their parents. Without
hesitation, we sit down and discuss what is going on.
We tell them, "You may not like what your parents say
or the rules of the home, but if your parents are working
hard to provide food, clothing, shelter, and discipline,
you should be obedient." We tell them they should take
themselves back home and apologize to their parents
and value what their parents are trying to instill into

them; it could save them in the long run.

I have a son who spent about nine years in prison. He took the advice of his grandmother, who told him when you reach eighteen years of age, you have the right to leave home because you are grown. On the day he turned eighteen, he packed up his clothes and left home. Unfortunately, his life went downhill from there. Sadly, it was prison that forced him to grow up and realize after confessing to his parents that he wished he had never listened to bad advice, but instead listened to the instructions of his parents.

Now that my son has been released from prison, he shares the importance of being obedient to parents, and tells children to be aware of both good and bad advice and to know the difference. God chastised him for his disobedience. Now my son sees the value of life and understands that he is blessed to have good parents who raised him in Christ. He took a wrong turn on that wide road called destruction.

"Train up a child in the way he should go; and when he is old, he will not depart from it." Proverbs 22:6

How is it a mother-in-law who had the best of everything from my husband and I could betray us? We provided my mother-in-law with vacations together and the remodeling of her home. Whatever was needed, we provided it for her. She got with family members and allowed them to put trash in her ears about us. How can you talk about your son's wife and think that he is supposed to overlook how you mistreat her? I did what I was supposed to do by loving her from a distance. I began to feel like the relationship was toxic and I had to break away. The hurt became unbearable. Sadly, our relationship has never been the same.

I applaud my husband. He is her son, but he has enough respect for his wife to be the husband that God made him to be for me. The Bible says in Proverbs 18:22, "He who finds a wife finds a good thing, and receives favor from the Lord." Wedding vows do not include husband, wife, and mother. I learned to bless my mother-in-law in spite of our problems. In-laws should know their place and stay in it to avoid confusion in the lives of their son- or daughter-in-law's family.

My husband vowed that he was going to take care of his family, and God blessed him to do just that. As parents, we tried our best to teach and raise our children by the Word of God. It is now time for the seeds that we have sown into their lives to manifest into good works.

"Do not be deceived: God is not mocked, for whatever one sows, that will he also reap."
Galatians 6:7

Our in-laws tried to teach our children to follow the ways of the world while we were fighting to get them to follow the ways of Christ. Our grandchildren have made their own decisions to keep their distance from the bitterness and deception. Satan is always lurking to see where there are gaps of confusion so that he can slip in and bring further destruction. Be careful of his devices of evil. During this period in my life, my faith was in Proverbs 4:23: "Above all else, guard your heart, for everything you do flows from it."

6

Biological Hurt

How does a mother feel when she is rejected by her own children? Let me explain why I ask this question. When God wants you to raise your children in Him, and the very ones you believe that should be supportive of that goal do the opposite, it can have a tremendous impact on your children. No family member should purposefully lead your children away from the godly values the parents are trying to instill in them.

It was troubling to witness family members who said that they loved the Lord and attended church every Sunday have such wicked hearts. Our children were fooled into believing ungodly teachings by their grandparents, aunts, uncles, and cousins. You should never tell someone else's children that it is okay to have sex outside of marriage or that it is okay to have a boyfriend or girlfriend at a young age. We didn't permit these things as their parents, knowing that their minds were in the developing stage and not mature enough to make sound decisions.

It takes a village to raise children – but beware of

the villagers! Identify and root out those who are not nurturing or giving wise counsel to your children. It was difficult for me to hear a grandmother say, "When my children got to be teenagers, I didn't make them go to church." This teaching was in direct violation of my and my husband's godly parenting for our children. My husband and I stood on the scripture that proclaimed, "As for me and my house, we will serve the Lord."

Our children rebelled against what we were teaching. They wanted the relaxed rules that Grandmother was advocating. They begin taking our business out of our home to family members. Those relatives were having open discussions with our children, who wanted to do what they wanted without any consequences. Instead of our family members being of one accord with us, they sided with our children and went against us as parents.

Sadly, our children felt empowered by those family members, regardless of what our rules were. There was also a spokesperson in our home influencing the other siblings to be disobedient. Not only were we having to deal with outside influence; we had inside influence, too. Satan was determined to destroy our family. Although their father and I were going through hell, together we stayed on our knees praying and worshipping God.

There were many nights as a mother I had to drink tears for water, knowing that Jesus was with us all the way. This was a reminder to me that I picked up my cross to follow Jesus and that there could never be a crown if I didn't go through life challenges and changes.

I believed that with Jesus helping me to bear my cross, things would get better. There were times in which I felt like giving up, but Jesus did not say every day was going to be sunny and bright. It was a bittersweet journey of pleasure and pain. Jesus said, "In this world we shall have tribulation, but be of good cheer for I have overcome the world."

I understood having a "thorn in my side" kept me on my knees praying. The lifestyles of some of our family members differed greatly from our moral value system. Some family members plotted, planned, deceived, and lied in an attempt to destroy my marriage and my family.

Just when we thought things could not get any worse, they did. We had relatives encouraging other family members to go to court to speak on our children's behalf to have one of them removed from the home. The Department of Human Services came to our home to do an investigation. When the social worker concluded her review, she said, "Mrs. Walker, they have too much."

It was frustrating and hurtful to see the children that we gave life to turn on us as if we were criminals and child abusers. Auspiciously, my son's plan did not work. The judge told the relative the reason my child wanted to stay with them was to run wild with no instructions or discipline. Family members had the nerve to tell us, "Sometimes you can be too strict."

Be careful of the seeds you plant and what you do to lead children astray. Trust me, God's word is not mocked. God tells us not to deceive little ones (Matthew 18:5-6). You will reap what you sow. Today, those family members who brought so much pain into our lives are catching hell at every turn. Their time to reap of their evil deeds have arrived.

Adding misery to misery, there were times our children did not want to be around us; they preferred being around deception and lies. Each child began to leave home, not knowing destruction was down the road. The most hurt a parent can experience is bringing children into the world, only for that child to turn on them because of strategically planned false information. The definition of strategy is "carefully designed or planned to serve a particular purpose or advantage." Family members purposely set out to bring down our home.

Many years went by, with two of my sons going to prison and the others not living up to their full potential in life. They must give an account to God for their disobedience and being part of the deception and lies that were told to them. As parents, we continue to pray for our children. It is our prayer that they will be delivered and the scales removed from their eyes. What has been put in them is the Word of God and their lives will turn back to serving Christ. We pray for the ones who misled and fooled them. Our longing for our children is to be led by the godly wisdom that we taught them.

7

Family Tree

How do you escape the madness that exists from a generation that is known for mental instability? What I mean is, how is it that every time something happens, we want to call it depression? Not everything is depression; it is those demons that we hold onto because of fear of being true to ourselves. Recognize that holding grudges and unforgiveness hurts us, not the person we are begrudging. We must begin making steps towards freeing ourselves from offenses that hamper our spiritual growth.

Holding offenses was something that I struggled with for a long time. Finally, I realized that I needed to let offenses go and move forward and live the abundant life that Christ wants me to live. I made the decision not to remain broken when Jesus has made me whole. Jesus laid down His life for me when He died on the cross for my sin. I ask you, "How long will you nurture your pain and brokenness?" For a long time, I felt as if I did not deserve to be loved because of my family's background.

I was a young girl from a broken home who had to figure things out for myself. Trying to make grown-up decisions was impossible. I stumbled through life making a lot of mistakes. With no direction on how to make good choices, I made a mess of my life. I was a child lost in the dark searching for light. At the age of 17, I began experiencing rejection and pain in ways no one should ever experience from those I trusted.

One day, the love of my life was introduced to me by a friend. This man did not have a clue what he was about to embark on. We started dating and it became clear to both of us that we wanted to be together. I did not want to mess up the relationship, so I did not disclose everything about me to him upfront. I struggled with how to tell him that I had two children, because I was afraid that he would reject me. Rejection had become the norm in my life.

I had to learn, "Never lie about your past." Tell the truth whether he or she stays or leaves. For years I was ashamed of my past, but not anymore. After I told him about my children, he accepted me and my children. Later, we had three more kids and we raised all of them as our own. Our love and determination were challenged at times because both of us were young and from broken homes. We had to grow up fast; there was no time to focus on ourselves. We made sure that no matter what, through the good, the bad and the ugly, we were going to stay together.

Without a father figure or role model in either home,

we struggled to figure out which way to go, being so young with a house full of kids. With the Lord's help and much prayer, we raised our children. If your father was missing from your life, it does not mean that you cannot be a good father and husband.

My husband was determined that he did not want to live his life after the example he observed from his father. He vowed when he became a man that he wanted to be a different type of father. He has kept that promise to himself.

I was ridiculed for having children before marriage. To my disappointment, I received a lot of harsh criticism and judgment. For years, I endured the nasty looks and the degrading words, but I prayed for my enemies. When you are a child of God, He will always protect you from those who are trying to destroy you. After much rain in my life, the SUN began to shine, and I was never the same again.

God is the lover of my life and redeemer of my soul. From a lost little girl who was not raised in church, meeting someone who knew Christ made a difference in my life. Lord, I am thankful for my husband for loving me through those days when I did not love myself.

I can honestly say that my husband is my soulmate. One should never give up on love because of what others may say. It does not matter what your family tree looks like. Shake off the negative opinions of others. I accepted my past and I am at peace with the consequences of my decisions.

God changed my life, and He can do the same for you. No longer am I a victim; I am an overcomer. I allowed the light of Christ to shine through me so that others can see Him in me. You can change, too. I have been where you may find yourself today. I know what it's like not to love yourself or allow others to love you.

As I studied God's word, I prayed and asked Him, "What is my purpose? Why is it taking so long for change to come into my life? Why am I not being blessed?" I asked those and many more questions. My insecurity immediately kicked in after I prayed, and I thought that my prayers were not going to be answered. To my surprise, God answered my prayers. The more I studied the Bible, the more God revealed to me that I must trust Him and stop relying on my own understanding.

Satan knows the blessings that God has for us, so he uses roadblocks to delay us from receiving God's best. Praise God that the spirit of the Lord has angels watching over us that know how to do spiritual warfare. We are children of the King. Our blessings cannot be stopped. What God has for you is for you and no one else.

It is so important to speak your goals and dreams into existence in your life and pray that His will be done for you. Ask God to order your footsteps. If you stumble and fall, get back up and keep moving forward.

8

Father, Where Are You?

The man I was told was my father was a pastor of two churches. I was born to parents who did not have a clue about the Lord. When my mother was pregnant with me, his beatings caused her to go into early labor with me. From what I was told, my mother married him because he was good-looking and wanted to leave the country life.

Not only did I have a father who did not take care of his family; his mother was adamant that I was not his child. My mother was always a sickly woman. When her health began to decline, he said to her, "You have lost your health and your husband." As my mother got worse, my grandmother, whom I loved dearly, came from Mississippi to Florida and took us home with her to take care of us.

The responsibility of a husband is to be the head of the household. If he is in Christ, he should be the provider and protector for his family. My father was never a father or husband. He did not take seriously the vows that said "...in sickness and in health."

Not everybody is marriage material. Ask God through prayer to reveal the character of the person you desire to marry. I would also suggest that you do a background check on the person you are planning to marry.

My father was not a good husband. Ironically, he ended up marrying my mom's best friend - the church secretary. I cannot be angry about that, but what I was angry about was the fact that I needed him in my life because of the hardships my mother faced. Coming from a family of seven was hard on my mother, especially since she was dealing with schizophrenia and other medical issues and frequently in and out of the hospital.

I was a lost child trying to understand why my family was not like other families with both a mother and a father working together as one. For years, I wondered what my life would have been like if both parents were in the home. I once heard my pastor say, "Having children is for grown folks, not children." Could it be that my parents had the age of adults, but the mind of children?

My mother was not perfect, either. She did the best that she could from what she had to deal with. I often saw and heard things that little girls should not see or hear. Many times, I came home to men in the house with Mom, drinking and partying. I remember one Friday I came home from school, and I saw a man, whom I had never seen before, beating my mother. You never know how much strength you have until you see someone hitting your mother. I pleaded with him to stop hitting her, but he did not listen. That is when I grabbed a baseball bat and started hitting him; suddenly the tables had turned, and he was pleading for me to stop hitting him. I told him to never hit a woman, especially my mother; she had been abused enough. I became my mother's protector, and I vowed no one would ever lay hands on her again.

My mother never got over the man who was supposed to be the superhero in our lives but instead turned out to be a nightmare. I must admit I hated my father for a long time, until I grasped that I was only hurting myself, not him. Once, he came to Mississippi and wanted to see me, but days went by before I could face him. Finally, I went to see him, and I could not say anything at first, because I was sizing him up and trying to figure out what in the world my mother saw in him, because I did not see anything in him worth having.

During our brief encounter, my father and I had a conversation that he did not want to have. I had so many questions he was not willing to answer. I learned that he was not seeking a relationship with his daughter whom he did not know. He needed money and a place to stay while he was in town. Yes, I determined he was a leech who pretended to be someone he was not; he did not even ask for forgiveness. It was then that I knew this man is not of God, but of Satan. God became my father. He has a love that will not turn or walk away. There is no greater love than that of the Lord.

9

Front Porch Gossipers

Front porch gossipers are folks who sit on the porch and gossip about everything and everybody. When they see you, they eat you up like a bag of Skittles. In order to become a member of the front porch gossipers, you must be a gossiper as well; peacemakers are not allowed. Front porch gossipers choose a topic, a person, or a thing to degrade. This becomes their full-time job, which they will never retire from if they are not willing to change. Front porch gossipers are busybodies. They are in everyone's business and wreak havoc in other people's lives. Stay away from front porch gossipers. Each front porch gossiper should have a sign on their door that says, "Mess Keeper...Beware."

Front porch gossipers have loose lips. They will tell everything. They do not know how to keep secrets, so do not share any confidential information around them. Front porch gossipers are happy to sow seeds of discord and divisiveness.

There is a lesson to be learned from the front porch gossipers. When mess-makers and gossipers approach you, look them in the eye and tell them, "Instead of using your mouth to hurt and destroy others, use it to encourage and uplift your brothers and sisters. Planting bad seeds will reap you a bad crop."

"A perverse person stirs up conflict and a gossiper separates close friends." Proverbs 16:28

Front porch gossipers carry out the devil's work. They gossip because they are angry, bitter, hateful, deceitful, and unhappy. They see the blessings of others, and they wonder why their own blessings never come.

My family and my husband's family felt that I was someone who had nothing and was nothing before I met him. I beg to differ; I was the child of a King before I met my husband. I came from royalty.

Never gossip about a person's past just because of where they are in their lives. Coming from an environment that showed me poverty and not beauty, what else was expected from a girl from the projects? Some said nothing good could come from the projects. I know that is not true. Today, I can tell you that the prize winners come from the projects, just like me, and I am not ashamed of where I came from.

Try a different approach to gossip: repent and change. Turn your life over to the one who created you to serve HIM.

10

I Am Free

I am free from the stronghold that kept me from being productive in life, by the help of God, counseling, close friends, my children, and a loving husband. I am able to view life from a different perspective than before. I have a new walk and a new talk, loving who I have become: a woman after God's heart, who is free to love without expecting anything in return.

I am not walking in doubt, hurt, or fear. Looking back over my life made me understand that I was my own enemy, allowing the fears of Satan to keep me in a dead state. My life was consumed, controlled, and yielded to him. Every day I was trying to figure out life, but I was doing it all wrong; I was doing it my way for years.

You cannot love anyone until you love yourself. I was so busy making everyone else happy that I forgot about my own happiness. It is important to take care of yourself and practice self-care. A wake-up call for me came when I understood that I was not properly taking care of myself physically, emotionally, or spiritually. Do not be fooled; I fooled myself about my health.

Keeping my mind in an unhappy place kept me physically sick. Covering up feelings that I never expressed unless I was pushed to anger was not healthy. Having no self-control and a killer tongue made me dangerous. Those who targeted me knew the only thing they had to do was to push the wrong button, and I would go from zero to a thousand. My advice to you is stop worrying over things and people that you have no control over. You cannot change others, but you can change you. Let go and let God do a new thing in you.

I was a volcano poised to erupt. Satan has ways of making us self-destruct if we are not strong enough to know which spirit we are dealing with. Carrying unhealthy emotions and feelings was not good for me. I had to find a better way to deal with anger. I began to open up about the past that haunted me for decades. I felt a release of pressure from my body when I decided to talk about my past.

The mother, sisters, and brothers that I longed for? God has blessed me with all that I needed and more. Although they are not biological, they are my spiritual brothers, sisters, and mothers in Christ. When I stopped looking at what I did not have and started focusing on what God has given me, I began thanking HIM for His many blessings.

Often times, my love and compassion were given and never returned. When I came into the knowledge of who I was, my life began to change. God has put Satan on notice. He says, "She is my daughter, and you no longer have power over her." As long as I live, I vow to fight for myself and others who deal with issues of life and to have compassion for those who will accept it.

For so long, I was angry with myself. Not only were people attacking me, but I was also attacking myself. Blaming myself for things that happened in my life that I had no control over. What do you do when you have isolated yourself from what is inside of you and is destined to come out? At that time, I could not figure it out. I repressed things in my mind, knowing all the time that if I kept ignoring my calling, life would not be the same for me. Nevertheless, it takes strength and inner courage to come out and face your demons.

I realized that I could not continue being scared to live my life. I learned to love myself. I now live my life through Jesus Christ. For all those who doubted me, I love you. For all those who said I was too old to be going to school, I love you. For all those who said you have been in school forever, I love you. For all those who hate me, I love you. For all those who said I would be just like my mother, I love you. Those who assaulted me, I forgive you.

Now that my path is clear and the scales have been removed from my eyes, I can see that it was never about me; it was about me picking up my cross and following the One who died for my sins. My Lord was not accepted by His own, so who am I? Am I any greater than my Father in heaven? No, Jesus went through more than I could have ever gone through.

Put on the whole armor of God to shield yourself from those fiery darts that will be thrown at you so they will not harm you. With Jesus holding my hand and guiding me, I can face tomorrow. Let me introduce to you this beautiful spirit that shines so bright and no longer hides in the night, afraid of the dark, because she was too weak to fight. That little girl is not afraid anymore. She is joyous, no longer filled with poisonous thoughts, because she was lost. She has scars and bruises; some visible, some not. The plot, the planning, was all designed for the sun to shine. No longer will darkness bear my name for the shame of my past. No longer am I tossed and driven by the winds of uncertainty.

I thank God for bringing me through the valley of the shadow of death so that I could share my story. For so long, I have been waiting with anticipation for the Shelia made in the image of Christ to appear. She has been hidden for a long time and preserved like a fine wine. She is loveable and kind. She could have given in and lost, but she turned to Jesus.

I am delivered and set free; I am a better person. The birthing experiences were difficult; nonetheless, in the end, God's plans for me prevailed.

As believers in Christ, we are living epistles being read by men. No matter what you go through, someone is watching how you handle yourself. Trust in the Lord. He will always bring you through every test, trial, and temptation. God wants to get the glory out of your life...let Him!

P.O. Box 453
Powder Springs, Georgia 30127
www.entegritypublishing.com
info@entegritypublishing.com
770.727.6517